CARTOON HOW-TO

Written by
Cyndie
Bellen-Berthézène

Illustrated by
Terry & Lisa Workman

SCHOLASTIC INC.

NEW YORK   TORONTO   LONDON   AUCKLAND   SYDNEY
MEXICO CITY   NEW DELHI   HONG KONG   BUENOS AIRES

ISBN 0-439-81332-8

Design by Emily Muschinske

Copyright © 2005 by HiArt! Inc. All rights reserved.
Published by Scholastic Inc.

SCHOLASTIC and associated logos are trademarks
and/or registered trademarks of Scholastic Inc.

HiArt! and associated logos are trademarks and/or registered trademarks of HiArt! Inc.

12 11 10 9 8 7 6 5 4 3 2 1   5 6 7 8 9 10/0

Printed in the U.S.A.
First Scholastic printing, October 2005

TABLE OF CONTENTS

This book is the real deal! Scholastic has teamed up with Cyndie Bellen-Berthézène, founder and director of **HiArt!**, one of the best children's art programs in Manhattan, to create this authentic and professional art book. *Cartoon How-To* was carefully crafted for kids just like you, and it includes tons of real drawing tips, easy to learn techniques, fun characters to draw, and inspiration to help you become an even better artist than you already are!

WELCOME! WELCOME! WELCOME TO CARTOONLAND

Cartoons and caricatures are everywhere, aren't they? They're in the books you read, the TV shows you watch, and even in newspapers and magazines. Look around as you walk down the street. You'll surely see cartoonish faces smiling down at you from giant posters all over town.

Right here in this handy book, you'll learn how to draw scads of cool, creative cartoons and—most importantly—you will find everything you'll need to create a 'Toonland of your very own. And then before you know it—**ZAP!**—you'll be drawing like a real cartoonist.

ON YOUR MARK,
GET SET,
GET DRAWING!

GETTING STARTED

THIS BOOK COMES WITH A PROFESSIONAL CARTOONING SUPPLY KIT. CHECK IT OUT!

Main Tool: 2B Pencil

You'll need a **2B pencil** (you probably have hundreds right in your very own home). Real cartoonists like to sketch with 2B because the markings don't get too smudgy. And with it, you'll be able to take your fabulous ideas and turn them into hilarious cartoons. Keep your pencil sharpened and your drawings will look really professional!

Eraser

The art kit includes a special **eraser**. Because it has fine, pointy edges, you'll be able to get rid of any teeny, tiny mistakes in your drawing—without making a mess of the whole picture. No fuss, no muss!

Marker

Once your sketch is finished, trace over the lines with your **waterproof black marker** (that's what makes that black outline you see around all cartoons). But it doesn't erase—EVER! So go slow and keep the cap on tight when you're not drawing. An ink spot on your rug will stay there forever.

Watercolor Pencils

Watercolor pencils are an incredible tool! Use them just like regular colored pencils. Then use a paintbrush to dab water over what you've drawn, and turn your pencil markings into paint. (How cool is that?!) Or, dip your pencil in a bit of water and draw with it wet. It creates a fantastic effect!

Paintbrush

A **paintbrush** helps bring color and beauty to your artwork—but don't drown it in water! If you leave a brush sitting in water for hours, it will fall apart. An inch or two of cool water in a cup is all you need to get started. Rinse your brush when you're done and make sure you leave it out to air dry.

Sketchpad

Your new **sketchpad** has bright, smooth paper—perfect for drawing. And your drawings will be safe and beautiful between its covers forever!

CHECKLIST

Now that you've got some artists' supplies, you'll want to set up an artist's workspace.

- ☑ Cover your work area with a mat or board. (Newspaper's not so great—the ink will rub off on your work and ruin it.)

- ☑ Find a safe place to store your supplies so they won't get lost.

- ☑ Make sure to wear an old shirt over your clothes so that you don't wreck them!

WHAT'S A CARICATURE ANYWAY?

You may not know even know what the word means, but believe it or not, you've already seen seventeen zillion of them. Caricatures are drawings that **EXAGGERATE** for a humorous effect. They take real things and make them either so **BIG** or so SMALL that you can't help laughing. For instance, pretend you go fishing and you catch one weenie little fish that's so tiny you don't even want to bother bringing it home. But you go to school the next day and tell everyone how you

THE WAY IT REALLY WAS

lucked out: The fish were biting like crazy, and your pail was so full that hundreds of fish were jumping out of the bucket onto the dock and into the air. That's called **exaggeration**.

THE EXAGGERATION

Caricatures do the same thing but they can exaggerate the way a person looks or moves, or even what they might be able to do. For example, let's say your friend Sarah's ninth birthday party is coming up and she's been nervous for days that she won't be able to blow out all ten candles at once. When the big moment arrives, all of her friends are there and everyone's excited. Normally, Sarah's a pretty calm and quiet kind of girl. (This is where the exaggeration comes in.) But suddenly, she takes a **H-U-U-U-U-GE** breath, and blows with all her might. A gigantic, powerful puff of air explodes from her mouth. She blows so hard that the whole top of the cake comes flying off—frosting, flowers, everything—all over her friends.

FROM CARICATURE TO CARTOON

Sarah is the perfect example of a caricature—we've taken the real Sarah and through exaggeration, we've completely changed our image of her.

The next step is to take this caricature technique and use it to create your own character. This character—totally invented by you—is called a **cartoon**. Cartoons are drawn almost the same way you draw caricatures. You might use some features of people and things familiar to you to help develop your cartoon character, but the beauty of the cartoon is that almost everything about the character really comes out of your own head. Your job as the cartoonist is to come up with the great idea.

So, let's say you want to develop a mean teacher for your main cartoon character. Think about all your teachers in school. Are there certain things you dislike about some of them? Make a list of things that bug you about your teachers:

1. _____

2. _____

3. _____

4. _____

5. _____

Take the traits you've written down, roll them into one person, and **VOILÀ!** One super-nasty cartoon teacher!

Now that you have the teacher's character down, what's the teacher's name? Names can be a great help in bringing your character to life. Suppose we take old super-nasty and call him **PROFESSOR PINKHAM, MOST EVIL TEACHER IN THE UNIVERSE!** It's a good name because it's made up of two words that add to his grossness: Pink and Ham! That way he can be very pink and very piggy. What will the name of your teacher be? Write it here:

_____

Lastly, every cartoon needs a few exaggerated details. So, for example, if **Professor Pinkham** wears thick glasses that are sometimes a little dirty, you would want to draw his glasses to be super big with huge, dirty blobs on them. Just the idea of Professor Pinkham, Most Evil Teacher in the Universe, will make everyone laugh because NOBODY is that creepy—except in cartoons. Think of some funny details about your teacher. What could you exaggerate? Write your ideas here:

1. _____

_____

2. _____

_____

3. _____

_____

4. _____

_____

Now try a fast drawing of what you think your character looks like on the facing page. Don't worry! Your drawing is going to be great. After all, it's YOURS!

How did your teacher come out?
No turning the page until you've
tried to draw your own teacher!

DRAWING PROFESSOR PINKHAM

Now, check out our Professor P! Does he look like what you thought he would? Check out his **BIG** body and his TEENY hands and feet!

Learning to draw this meanie will teach you some really good tricks for drawing caricatures. Pull out your sketchbook and follow these simple step-by-steps. Combine the tricks you learn here with what you did on your own, and you'll be well on your way to cartoon mastery!

Step 1: Always start with a basic shape! Artists use very lightly drawn guidelines to help plan out the face.

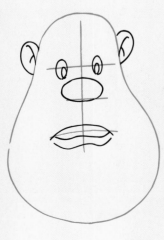

Step 2: Begin by drawing his ear. It's two little lines—like a lopsided T surrounded by half a heart. The eyes are ovals with littler ovals inside. His piggy nose sits right on the center line. The mouth is like an upside down smile attached to a hot dog.

Step 3: Erase the guidelines, being careful not to erase any of your drawing. The hair should look like a leaf with too many edges. Draw an upside down U for the tongue. Draw tiny U's for the Professor's Halloween teeth.

Step 4: Erase the head guideline peeking through the hair. Add tiny curved lines around the eyes, nose, and mouth. They give Pinkham's face its character. Loopy O's make great nostrils.

Step 5: Now, draw his glasses! Notice how the inside corners are hidden behind his nose. Next, add his eyebrows. They should be meanie-looking brows; one up, one down. Trace over the mustache shown here to get the feel for drawing hairy things.

Step 6: Now carefully, use your black marker to ink over your drawing. Use your eraser to get rid of any leftover pencil lines.

Step 7: It's time to color! You may want to make yourself a couple of Xerox copies before you start coloring. That way, if you don't like what you do, you can just start again!

Step 8: Add Pinkham's body to his head by drawing his basic stick figure. Everywhere his body bends (at the joints) draw a tiny circle—it will help you later.

Step 9: Draw Pinkham's pear-shaped body, taking note that his jaw is so huge and his body is so fat, that we can't see his neck!

Step 10: Now fill out the rest of his shape by drawing his chubby arms and legs! Like your arms, the big muscle is on top and your wrist is little. Then do the same thing for the legs, making a slight U shape for his waist.

Step 11: Erase your body guidelines. Now it's time to dress this guy! Draw the wings of his collar around the neck, and make the shape of the tie like a triangle for the knot and a diamond for the tie. Then add a squiggle for the skinny part of the tie. Add his pocket full of supplies.

Step 12: Pinkham needs some wrinkles to make his clothing look like he's really fat. Add wrinkles at the elbows, armpits, and waist. Then turn the basic hand and shoe shapes into something all your friends will recognize.

Step 13: Carefully use your black marker to ink over your drawing. Use your special eraser to get rid of any leftover pencil lines.

Step 14: Just like for the head, make Xerox copies of your drawing before you color. Then experiment with color to your heart's content!

Wow! You just drew your first caricature! And without using a single word, your picture tells a pretty detailed story. Cool, huh?

GETTING A HEAD

Now that you've learned the basics of caricature and cartooning, it's time for some cartooning tips that can make your drawings the best they can be. And there's no better place to start than from the top!

Cartoon heads are made from simple shapes: Circles, ovals, cylinders, triangles, and even squares. As a beginning cartoonist, you may think all heads are the same shape—like an egg, for instance. But cartoonists will often join two shapes (or more): A circle overlapping with an oval, for example. The circle gives you a big forehead (that can be for your brainy characters) and the oval a long, funny jaw.

There's a pretty standard formula for how to make a realistic face. It goes like this:

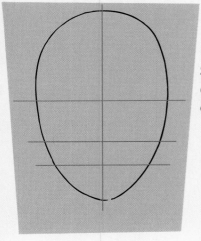

Step 1: Draw an oval, adding light guidelines.

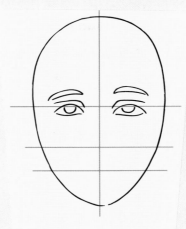

Step 2: The eyes are halfway between the top of the head and the chin. Don't forget the eyebrows!

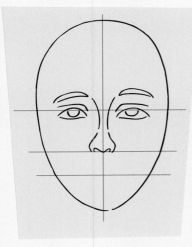

Step 3: The bottom of the nose is halfway between the eyes and the chin.

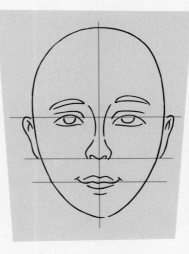

Step 4: The mouth is halfway between the nose and the chin. The ears are even with the nose.

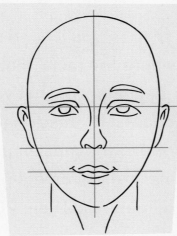

Step 5: Add the neck and violà!

But cartoon faces don't try to look "realistic"—they look funny. To do that, cartoonists move the proportions of the standard face around. For example, we expect people's eyes to look a certain way. When the eyes are just slits or beady little things, they look funny. Maybe you'll make your character's eyes very small and high, or the mouth all the way down at the chin. Think about it and see what you can come up with!

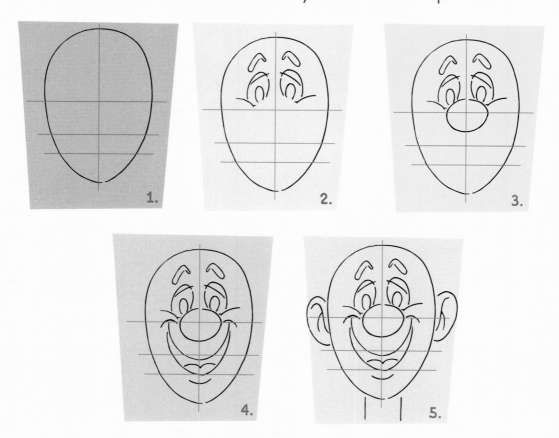

Once you've drawn your starting shapes, you'll need to sketch some light guidelines to help you figure out where the facial features should go. You might think guidelines are just for beginners or that you don't really need them—but that's untrue on both counts! Professional cartoonists use them all the time. Guidelines are one of the most important tricks of the trade. They'll help you fit everything into its correct place. When your drawing is finished, erase the guidelines. And then, POOF! Your drawing turns into a real, live cartoon!

Let's practice some head construction taking it step-by-step, nice and slow, by creating the Cartoonland kids. These instructions will teach you how to draw both boys and girls easily.

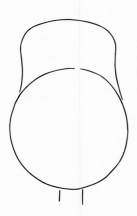

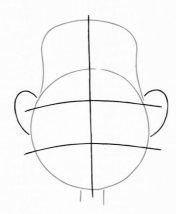

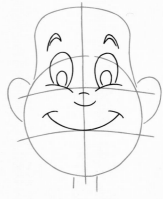

Step 1: Start with the big shapes. A circle for his face, a funny bump on top for his skull and hair, and two lines for his neck.

Step 2: Now add your guidelines in light pencil. Using the guidelines, draw ears which are like the letter C.

Step 3: Draw two cheeklines. Then for eyes, draw upside down U's with little U's inside them. Teeny boomerangs above the eyes make good brows. The nose is a tiny curved line with an upturned U below it. Make the top lip a big smile stretching almost from ear to ear, with two curved lines at each corner.

Step 4: Now add the hair shape around the skull. Add a slice of watermelon for the bottom of the mouth. His chin is a small line that matches the curve of the mouth. Add a small line inside his mouth for teeth. Follow the curve of the ears to make the inside of them. Then, carefully erase the guidelines.

Step 5: The front of the hair is made from a shallow 3 shape. Finish off the eyes: See how the eyelids extend right beyond the eye itself? Don't forget the eyeballs! Put a small upside down U inside the mouth for the tongue.

Step 6: Whew! Now add a bunch of snaky lines for hair. Also, give his skinny neck a double ring for the T-shirt.

Step 7: And now, ink away! Carefully erase the remaining pencil lines.

Step 8: Before you color, make a few Xerox copies of your drawing. Then you can really experiment with how you want him to look.

Now let's draw the girl. This time the face is an oval. Take a good look at her. She's turned to the side. Follow these steps carefully and you'll soon become an expert in the three-quarter profile.

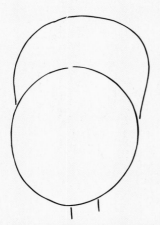 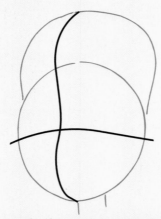 

Step 1: Start with an oval for the face. Add an arc for the skull. Then add two straight lines for the neck.

Step 2: Now add guidelines in light pencil. Her head is turned toward the left, so the vertical guideline is going to be closer to the left side of her face.

Step 3: Draw a little curve for the top of the nose and a bigger curve for the bottom. Add upturned cheeklines, then rest her big U-shaped eyes on them. Add backward C's for pupils. Little boomerangs at the top of the oval make nice brows. Draw the mouth line so it's wider on the right side, with smile lines at each corner.

Step 4: Now erase the guidelines on her face. Draw the big hair shape around the skull. See how the right side of her hair angles up? The eyelashes are made with slanted lines. The bottom part of the mouth is a U-shape and her chin line should match the curve of her nose.

Step 5: Add details to the hair using curved lines. Draw the tongue and teeth by adding two little arcs inside her mouth. At the bottom of her neck, add a double ring for the collar.

Step 6: Erase the remaining guidelines and any extra pencil lines. Ink the whole drawing except the hair details. You'll use colored marker to ink those lines.

Step 7: Make a few Xerox copies of your drawing and get coloring! To challenge yourself, check out where the shadows fall on her face, neck, and hair. Try a slightly darker color or add a little pencil over your color to give it a shadowy feeling. You can smudge the pencil gently with your finger so that it blends into the color.

TIMES TWO

Now that you've learned how to draw a cartoon head from the front and in three-quarter profile, you're ready for a fantastic cartoon trick: **THE DOUBLE TAKE**. (You'll wow your friends with this one!) Double takes happen all the time in real life. You're racing to do something, you pass by something weird without paying attention, and right after you go by it, your brain screams: **WHAT WAS THAT?!**

So for example, let's say you're in a hurry to get home to walk your dog, when you pass your best friend tossing a ball back and forth with someone. You say hi without stopping and as soon as you've passed him, you realize he's playing catch with a **GHOST**. You turn your head back around at top speed to check out the scene again, because you think you're losing you're mind. That's the double take!

Here's how to draw a double take. Let's begin by practicing the three different perspectives, before putting it all together.

Step 1: First, practice the profile. Draw your basic shapes and add guidelines. (Note: You only see one eye!) The nose is a triangle that sticks out at the center guideline. A gentle S shape makes the open mouth, showing the teeth and tongue. See how the left side of her hair looks like half a Christmas tree?

Step 2: Once you've erased your guidelines and inked the sketch over, your profile should look like this.

Step 3: Now let's draw the front view. This should be easy after Professor P and the boy's head. Remember to start with your basic shapes and guidelines, and then add all of her features. Take note of her wide-open mouth.

Step 4: Once you've erased your guidelines and inked the sketch over, your front view should look like this.

Step 5: Lastly, practice your $^3/_4$ views. Check out pages 22 to 23 if you need a refresher on how to do this.

Step 6: Once you've erased your guidelines and inked the sketch over, your $^3/_4$ view should look like this.

Great job! Now you're ready to draw the double-take faces all together!

Step 1: Begin with the front view of her face in the center of your paper, not drawing all of her hair.

Step 2: Add two $^3/_4$ views, one on each side. See how they grow right out of the central head? The best way to do this is to draw the full head shapes and then just erase the parts that overlap. If you don't put the whole head in at first, you might end up with faces that are too skinny or weird.

Step 3: Add one profile head on each side of the three heads you've drawn so far. You'll only need half a triangle of hair on each side.

Step 4: Now add movement! Draw a few pairs of curved lines to make it look like she's moving really fast. She's so shocked that sweat flies off of her head. Some little sweat drops will do the trick.

Step 5: Then it's time to ink, and then...

Step 6: COLOR!

And there you have it: A fantastically professional double-take!

LET'S FACE IT!

The last thing you need for your character's head is an **EXPRESSION**. Is your character mad, sad, glad, bad, shocked, vomiting, terrified, bored, sleepy or . . . ? Think about what you want your character to be feeling. Then, you'll need to adapt the features you drew in the step-by-steps to show that character's expression.

Let's practice drawing some expressions! First, check out these four basic expressions:

MAD

SAD

SCARED

HAPPY

If you were to draw these expressions, would you draw them the same way or change them? Here's your chance! Fill in the four blank heads below with your own versions of mad, sad, scared, and happy. You can copy what we've done, or draw your own from scratch!

MAD

SAD

SCARED

HAPPY

Now let's take expressions to the next level and have some fun! A great way to get ideas is to look at yourself in a mirror and see what kinds of expressions you can come up with. Here are some ideas:

BAD SMELL

SNEAKY

SHOCKED

SILLY

Use these blank faces to draw your own expressions—again, either copying ours or drawing your own. Then on the line underneath each head, write the title of your expression.

bad smell

sneaky

shocked

silly

MOVIN' ON UP

Now it's time for our characters to get out there in the world and strut their stuff!

'Toonland isn't just a cool drawing. It's filled with real characters doing their thing. Check it out! There's a whole story in the works and things are really hopping!

In Cartoonland, there are characters (and creatures) of all kinds. And just by observing their expressions and body language, we get a pretty good idea of what they're up to. Turn back to the picture and look at it again. Then make a list of your favorite characters from the picture, mentioning what they're doing and how they're feeling. Give each character a name that you think fits with the way they look.

1. _____

_____

2. _____

_____

3. _____

_____

4. _____

_____

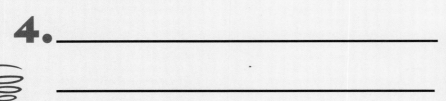

Did you see the happy cactus? Did you find the alien's spacecraft? Who do you think is running in the background? It's easy to make up stories about them, isn't it? That's because the movements their bodies are making—their **GESTURES**—give us clues about who they are. Take a look at your family and friends.

Do you recognize them coming toward you before you can see their faces? Sure you do. You can tell by something as simple as the way they walk—whether they slouch with their hands in their pockets all the time, or do nothing but jump up and down like a jumping bean. You can easily tell who people are by their body language.

So to create your cartoon character, you're going to need to pick out some body language for them. Does your character throw her head back when she laughs? Does he stomp around when he's angry? Or does your character like to cartwheel down the street?

Remember those stick figures you used to draw when you were in kindergarten? Well, look at this!

A stick figure is not just a little kid's drawing. It's a tool to help you imagine your person's skeleton in motion. Hello, bones! You need to figure out how those bones move in order to give your person a recognizable attitude.

It's time to go back to the mirror! Look at your body in the mirror as you make a big gesture. Is your head straight or leaning to one side? Where are you arms? How about your feet? Which way are they pointing? Is your spine straight? Take your pencil and make a few stick figures of yourself.

You can also get a friend or family member to make some gestures for you. You can even play a game where you call out an attitude—say, bossy—and the other person does the gesture while you have one minute (you can use a timer, too!) to draw your stick figure. Take turns! The more stick figures you make, the better you'll become at drawing gestures. Since you'll want to do lots of drawings, you might choose to use regular paper, rather than your sketchbook. That way you can draw hundreds of them!

Another way to get your stick figure skills going is to take a magazine and find a person whose pose or gesture you really like. Then take a piece of paper you can kind of see-through, and place it on top of the picture in the magazine. Do you see the person's body through your paper? Now draw their stick figure on to your paper with your marker. Then try the same stick figure again, without the magazine.

Draw a zillion different gestures for your character until you know you've got it down.

SKETCH TIME!

Drumroll, please! It's time to draw! How about the Cartoonland kids? Sounds like a big project? Not at all. It's easy!

Step 1: Start with your stick figures. Little circles at the joints show where the body bends.

Step 2: Add the skull shape and guidelines for the face. Use curved guidelines for the views of the face that aren't straight on. The eyeline is halfway down from the top of the skull and the bottom half of the face divides in thirds.

Step 3: The eyes, nose, and mouth are all easy curves. See how they sit right on the guidelines? The girl's eyes are upside down U's on a small smiley shape and the boy's eyes loop around so that they're all one piece. Don't forget the eyebrows!

Step 4: Some nice, fluffy hair follows just outside of the skull shape you drew in Step 2. We see the boy's whole ear from the side, which is a backwards C.

Step 5: Finish the boy's ear with a relaxed, sideways E. Teeth are just a simple line that mirrors the upper lip shape, and tongues are tiny upside down U's. See how the boy's neck follows the curve of his spine? Don't forget the boy's eyelids, the girl's eyelashes, and their face outlines.

Step 6: And now for the big shapes of the body. An oval for the hip joints with a rectangular body.

Step 7: Follow the stick figure curves for the arms and legs. Little U's for the kneebends go right below the joints. Don't forget a gentle L for her ankle.

Step 8: Add fingers and toes to their hands and her feet. Each of the finger ovals should be about the same thickness and the tips should line up. Look at your own hands and look at the shape outlined by your fingertips. They make a nice semi-circle, don't they?

Step 9: Erase the guidelines and then dress 'em up! See how the clothes are wider than the body? Draw in lines where the clothes are stretching from the kids' movements.

Step 10: Finish off the shoes, and now you can erase the body lines inside their clothes.

Step 11: Now turn the water on! The nozzle is tricky—look carefully: It's a bunch of backwards C's with a little J in the middle. The water comes out in a big V, and each of the water blobs follows a straight line out of the nozzle. Leave space in between the spurts to make it feel like the water is rushing out of the hose.

Step 12: INK away and erase any leftover guidelines. Make a few Xerox copies of the finished drawing so you can...

Step 13: COLOR! See what you can do with the darker shadows on their clothes and hair. Did you notice that his jeans have worn out knees? And don't forget the little white spots of his pupils.

CREATURES, CRITTERS & CREEPY CRAWLERS

Spice up your cartoons with a few **MONSTERS**! Learning how to draw people is a crucial part of cartooning, but it's also important to let your imagination run wild. Monsters can add suspense, horror, or just plain **FUN** to your cartoons.

Think about it: A creature appears out of nowhere. We see it quietly, tapping the unsuspecting boy on the shoulder from behind. The boy— who thinks that the tapping is just his mom reminding him to finish his homework—turns around to grumble about being too tired to do any more work when ... **YAAAAAAAOOOOOOOWWWWW! A MONSTER!**

So, let's get started with the basics of monster-making. Before you jump into creating your own critters, follow these steps to recreate this Cartoonland creature. It'll give you a taste for monster magic!

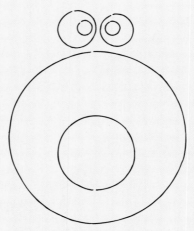

Step 1: **Start with the big shapes: 6 circles.**

Step 2: Draw boomerang-shaped eye sockets for the monster. Also, add a nice little triangle with no bottom for the top of the nose, and triangles that wiggle on the sides for ears. An overgrown U and some little cheek lines make the top part of a friendly monster smile.

Step 3: Make the eyes see; add little circles inside the circles. Connect the eyes to the head with two pairs of curved lines that look like skinny necks. Draw two beak-shaped triangles for the sides of the nose. Add a whole bunch of goofy triangles for the teeth.

Step 4: Boomerangs again—this time for the eyebrows. Put little curved lines under the eyes. Follow the curves for the lines inside the ears. Add a pair of U's for the bottom of the mouth. And don't forget two little circles in the middle of his nose so he can breathe.

Step 5: Add some leafy fur right inside the big body circle. Also, his tongue is just a flattened out 3. Add three more goofy triangles inside the bottom of the mouth for teeth. (Not too sharp!)

Step 6: This is a quicky: The leg bones. A nice circle for the knee cap and then a long leg—curving in—kind of bow-legged. And the feet are just triangles that look like big chocolate kisses.

Step 7: Erase the body guidelines—the big circle you started with. Then add toes. You'll need four circles. See how the right and left toes are only partial circles? Between them, you'll need some foot bones.

Step 8: Put some meat on those skinny legs! Add a balloon-shaped toenail to each toe. See how the left and right toenails are off to the sides of the circles?

Step 9: Turn those funny feet into claws. Erase the top part of the toe circles—not the part that joins to the foot bones—and then fix 'em up.

Step 10: Now, ink over your monster, looking to see which lines are thicker and which are thinner. Experiment! Also, carefully erase any remaining guidelines and pencil markings.

Step 11: COLOR!

MAKE YOUR OWN MONSTER

Not all monsters need to be scary. They can be funny, silly, and wacky, too! It's easy to envision a group of gigantic, hairy—but friendly—monsters, all dressed up in their monster finest, having a monster tea party. They might even have a monster butler serving them tea!

Incorporate basic shapes, stick figures, and/or wacky expressions in your monster cartoon. The tricks you learned to create people also apply to making your monster! What kind of monsters will come to tea at YOUR house? Are they small and furry with giant ears? Are they pink and fluffy?

Or are they big, hairy, growly, and wearing overalls and giant boots that make a ton of noise with every step they take? **ROAR!**

Imagination time! Just let the ideas roll from one to the next, like water pouring out of your kitchen faucet. Take the first idea that comes to your mind, say a furry beast, and add the very next thing you think of, like a million legs. Then each leg gets a shoe. And since the little beast is so well dressed, let's add a hat. And let's give him a cane and make him a Broadway star. Which means he has to sing and dance. Let your imagination run wild!

Decide what your monster should look like, what it should be doing, what kind of voice it has, and what it's wearing. Make lists to keep track of all your new monster ideas. Once you have your monster's characteristics down on paper, you can even mix and match them.

Physical Features	Personality Traits	Clothing	Actions

ALL GOOD THINGS DON'T COME TO AN END!

While our book has come to an end, Cartoonland is here to stay! Drawing, inventing, and cartooning come out of your imagination—a special world which never shuts down. With the cartooning skills you've learned, you'll be able to invent endless new friends and creatures. The more you draw, the easier and easier the tricks you've learned will become. Pretty soon, you'll find yourself striking out on your own, inventing whole new colorful worlds of hilarious cartoons to dazzle your family and friends. Come back to this book any time you want to review something. In the meantime,

MAY THE 'TOON BE WITH YOU!